PRINCEWILL LAGANG

Building a Strong Foundation: The Early Years of Marriage

First published by PRINCEWILL LAGANG 2023

Copyright © 2023 by Princewill Lagang

All rights reserved. No part of this publication may be reproduced, stored or transmitted in any form or by any means, electronic, mechanical, photocopying, recording, scanning, or otherwise without written permission from the publisher. It is illegal to copy this book, post it to a website, or distribute it by any other means without permission.

Princewill Lagang asserts the moral right to be identified as the author of this work.

First edition

*This book was professionally typeset on Reedsy.
Find out more at reedsy.com*

Contents

1	Introduction	1
2	The Transition to Marriage	3
3	Effective Communication	6
4	Shared Goals and Values	9
5	Navigating Finances Together	12
6	Intimacy and Emotional Connection	15
7	Balancing Independence and Togetherness	18
8	Dealing with Family and In-Laws	21
9	Handling Life Transitions	24
10	Conflict Resolution Strategies	27
11	Fostering Mutual Growth	30
12	Celebrating Milestones and Looking Forward	33

1

Introduction

In the journey of love, companionship, and commitment, the early years of marriage stand as a pivotal period that lays the foundation for a lasting partnership. This book delves into the significance of these initial years, exploring how the choices, habits, and dynamics established during this time can profoundly shape the trajectory of a marriage.

Marriage is often perceived as the union of two individuals, but it is also the amalgamation of two unique histories, backgrounds, and ways of life. The intertwining of these factors can create both opportunities and challenges, especially during the formative phase. As couples navigate this juncture, they have the chance to establish patterns of communication, trust, and understanding that will shape the course of their relationship.

The importance of a solid groundwork during these early years cannot be overstated. Just as a strong foundation supports the weight of a building, a well-nurtured partnership can withstand the trials and tribulations that life inevitably presents. Conversely, neglecting this phase may lead to misunderstandings, resentment, and even the unraveling of what could have been a deep and lasting connection.

In this book, we will explore the multifaceted aspects of building a strong foundation during the initial years of marriage. From effective communication strategies and conflict resolution techniques to shared goals and individual growth, each facet contributes to the overall strength and resilience of the relationship. Drawing from both research and real-life stories, we will delve into the complexities of these early years, offering insights and practical advice for couples seeking to lay a meaningful and enduring groundwork.

As we embark on this journey of exploration and introspection, it is our hope that readers will gain a deeper understanding of the critical role played by the early years of marriage. By recognizing the significance of this phase and actively working to establish a solid foundation, couples can pave the way for a partnership that not only withstands the test of time but also thrives and flourishes amid life's challenges.

2

The Transition to Marriage

The Transition from dating to married life marks a significant juncture in the journey of a couple. It is a phase characterized by a blend of excitement, anticipation, and a touch of uncertainty as two individuals evolve from being romantically involved to becoming life partners. In this chapter, we will delve into the intricate dynamics of this transition, examining the various changes and adjustments that define this phase of a relationship.

2.1 Embracing Change and Uncertainty

As couples make the leap from dating to marriage, they embark on a path of transformation. The dynamics of the relationship shift, and both individuals are tasked with adapting to new roles and responsibilities. The familiar patterns of dating give way to a more intertwined existence, where decisions are made collectively, and actions have repercussions that extend beyond the individual.

2.2 Redefining Identity and Roles

The transition to marriage prompts a reevaluation of individual identities and roles. Each partner must navigate the balance between maintaining a sense of self and embracing the shared identity of a couple. Questions may arise about autonomy, personal goals, and the compromises required to build a harmonious partnership.

2.3 Communication and Conflict Resolution

Effective communication becomes paramount during this phase. Couples must learn to express their thoughts, feelings, and expectations openly and honestly. Additionally, conflict resolution skills take on a new level of importance, as differences and disagreements arise more frequently in the context of shared responsibilities and decision-making.

2.4 Navigating Intimacy and Emotional Closeness

Intimacy takes on a multifaceted dimension as couples transition to marriage. Emotional closeness deepens as partners share not only positive experiences but also vulnerabilities and challenges. Physical intimacy may also evolve, influenced by factors such as stress, exhaustion, and the demands of daily life.

2.5 Adjusting to Domestic Life

Married life often entails sharing a living space, which can be a significant adjustment. The mundane aspects of daily routines, household chores, and financial management require coordination and compromise. These seemingly small tasks can impact the overall harmony of the relationship.

2.6 Building a Strong Support System

The transition to marriage is also an opportunity to establish a broader support network. Couples may find solace in connecting with other married couples, seeking guidance from mentors, or even engaging in counseling to navigate challenges effectively.

2.7 Embracing Growth and Flexibility

Flexibility becomes a key attribute as couples adapt to the changing landscape of marriage. Individuals evolve over time, influenced by personal experiences and external factors. Embracing growth, both individually and as a couple, allows for the continued development of the partnership.

In navigating the transition from dating to marriage, couples embark on a journey of growth, exploration, and mutual understanding. The changes and adjustments that define this phase may present challenges, but they also offer opportunities for deepening the connection and building a resilient foundation. Through effective communication, shared values, and a willingness to adapt, couples can navigate this transition with grace and set the stage for a fulfilling and enduring marital journey.

3

Effective Communication

Communication forms the bedrock of any successful relationship, and in the context of marriage, it takes on even greater significance. This chapter delves into the vital role of open and respectful communication in building a strong foundation for a lasting partnership. We will explore strategies that encompass active listening, the art of expressing feelings, and the resolution of conflicts.

3.1 The Foundation of Open Communication

Open communication is the cornerstone of a healthy marriage. It involves sharing thoughts, emotions, and ideas without fear of judgment or reprisal. Through open communication, couples cultivate a sense of understanding and connection, fostering an environment where both partners feel heard and valued.

3.2 The Power of Active Listening

Active listening is an essential skill for effective communication. It entails giving one's full attention to the speaker, seeking to understand their perspective before formulating a response. By practicing active listening, couples can minimize misunderstandings, demonstrate empathy, and demonstrate a genuine interest in each other's thoughts and feelings.

3.3 Expressing Feelings with Honesty and Empathy

The ability to express feelings honestly yet empathetically is a hallmark of healthy communication. Sharing emotions openly creates a space for vulnerability and deepens the emotional bond between partners. However, it's important to convey feelings in a manner that encourages understanding rather than defensiveness.

3.4 Navigating Conflicts Constructively

Conflicts are a natural part of any relationship, but how they are managed can greatly impact the partnership. Constructive conflict resolution involves addressing issues without blame or hostility. Couples can achieve this by focusing on the problem at hand, using "I" statements to express concerns, and working collaboratively toward solutions that meet both partners' needs.

3.5 Timing and Environment Matter

Effective communication is not just about what is said, but also when and where it is said. Choosing the right time and creating a conducive environment can enhance the receptivity of the listener. Avoid discussing sensitive topics in the heat of the moment or in public settings, as this can hinder productive communication.

3.6 Nonverbal Communication and Cues

Nonverbal cues, such as facial expressions, body language, and tone of voice, play a significant role in communication. Partners should be attuned to these cues, as they often convey emotions that words may not. Being mindful of nonverbal communication helps prevent misunderstandings and encourages genuine connection.

3.7 Seeking Professional Help

In cases where communication challenges persist, seeking the guidance of a professional, such as a marriage counselor or therapist, can be immensely beneficial. These experts offer unbiased perspectives, teach valuable communication techniques, and provide a safe space for couples to navigate complex issues.

By mastering the art of effective communication, couples can create a nurturing and supportive atmosphere in their marriage. Open communication fosters understanding, prevents misunderstandings, and strengthens the emotional connection. The strategies outlined in this chapter empower couples to listen actively, express themselves authentically, and resolve conflicts with grace. Through this commitment to healthy communication, couples lay the groundwork for a partnership that thrives on mutual respect, understanding, and enduring love.

4

Shared Goals and Values

In the intricate tapestry of marriage, the threads of shared goals and values weave a strong and resilient bond. This chapter delves into the profound significance of aligning aspirations and values as a couple, illustrating how this alignment contributes to a profound sense of unity and purpose within the partnership.

4.1 The Essence of Shared Goals and Values

Shared goals and values form the bedrock upon which a meaningful and enduring partnership is built. Goals are the compass points that guide a couple's journey, while values provide the moral and ethical framework that shapes their decisions and interactions. Aligning these elements creates a roadmap for the couple's collective growth and fulfillment.

4.2 Building a Sense of Unity

When partners share goals and values, they create a sense of unity that transcends the sum of their individual parts. This unity fosters a deep connection, as both individuals work together toward a common purpose. It nurtures a feeling of being in sync, which in turn strengthens emotional intimacy and mutual support.

4.3 Navigating Life's Challenges

Shared goals and values act as a source of strength during challenging times. When couples face adversity, their common aspirations remind them of their shared purpose and motivate them to overcome obstacles. The sense of unity that emerges from shared goals reinforces the couple's ability to weather life's storms together.

4.4 Alignment and Decision-Making

Aligning goals and values streamlines decision-making, making it easier for couples to choose paths that honor their shared aspirations. Whether making financial decisions, career choices, or lifestyle changes, couples with aligned goals find it easier to make choices that resonate with both partners' desires.

4.5 Cultivating Mutual Growth

The pursuit of shared goals encourages couples to grow together, fostering an environment where each partner's personal development contributes to the betterment of the partnership. As individuals evolve and learn, their growth is interwoven with the growth of the relationship, resulting in a dynamic and thriving partnership.

4.6 Communication and Compromise

Effectively aligning goals and values requires open communication and a willingness to compromise. Partners should openly discuss their aspirations and values, seeking common ground and understanding where differences lie. Compromise ensures that both individuals feel heard and valued, fostering a harmonious path forward.

4.7 Nurturing Shared Experiences

Shared goals and values also lead to shared experiences, which further cement the bond between partners. Collaborating on projects, embarking on adventures, and celebrating achievements together create lasting memories that strengthen the emotional connection and contribute to the richness of the relationship.

By aligning their goals and values, couples create a roadmap for shared growth, purpose, and fulfillment. The unity forged through this alignment empowers couples to navigate challenges, make decisions, and experience life's joys together. As couples nurture their shared aspirations, they lay a foundation for a marriage that thrives on mutual understanding, collaboration, and a deeply rooted sense of togetherness.

5

Navigating Finances Together

The journey of marriage is not only an emotional union but also a financial partnership. The early years of marriage are a crucial period for couples to establish a solid financial foundation. This chapter delves into the complexities of financial challenges and strategies that couples encounter during this phase. It addresses budgeting, setting shared financial goals, and effectively navigating money-related conflicts.

5.1 The Intersection of Finances and Marriage

The merging of two lives also involves the merging of two financial histories. Early in marriage, couples must navigate the transition from separate financial identities to a shared financial journey. This transition requires open communication and a willingness to work together.

5.2 The Importance of Budgeting

Budgeting is a cornerstone of responsible financial management. It involves tracking income and expenses, setting priorities, and making informed decisions about spending. Creating a joint budget helps couples understand their financial situation, allocate resources effectively, and avoid unnecessary stress.

5.3 Setting Shared Financial Goals

Shared financial goals provide couples with a sense of purpose and direction. Whether saving for a home, planning for children's education, or investing for retirement, these goals encourage collaboration and mutual motivation. Jointly working towards these aspirations enhances the feeling of partnership.

5.4 Open Communication About Money

Transparent and honest communication about money is essential in a marriage. Partners should openly discuss their financial expectations, attitudes, and past experiences. This dialogue helps uncover potential sources of conflict and allows for compromise and mutual understanding.

5.5 Addressing Money-Related Conflicts

Money-related conflicts are common in many marriages. These conflicts often stem from differences in spending habits, financial priorities, and expectations. Couples should address these conflicts through active listening, empathy, and finding solutions that honor both partners' perspectives.

5.6 Equal Contributions and Responsibilities

Discussing how financial contributions and responsibilities will be shared is crucial. Couples must determine whether they will pool their income, maintain separate accounts, or adopt a combination of both approaches. It's important to find an arrangement that aligns with both partners' values and preferences.

5.7 Building an Emergency Fund

An emergency fund is a vital safety net for unexpected expenses or financial hardships. Establishing and contributing to this fund is essential for financial stability and peace of mind. It helps prevent the need to rely on credit and ensures the couple is prepared for unforeseen challenges.

5.8 Seeking Professional Financial Advice

If navigating finances becomes particularly challenging, seeking the guidance of a financial advisor can be valuable. Advisors can help couples create a tailored financial plan, address complex issues, and provide insights to make informed decisions.

Navigating finances together in the early years of marriage requires a combination of communication, collaboration, and commitment. By embracing budgeting, setting shared financial goals, and addressing conflicts openly, couples can lay the groundwork for a financially stable and harmonious partnership. The decisions made during this phase not only impact the present but also set the stage for a secure and prosperous future together.

6

Intimacy and Emotional Connection

In the intricate tapestry of marriage, intimacy forms the threads that bind couples together in a profound and meaningful way. This chapter delves into the multifaceted role of both physical and emotional intimacy in fostering marital satisfaction. We will explore how couples can maintain and nurture their closeness to create a lasting and fulfilling partnership.

6.1 The Significance of Intimacy

Intimacy encompasses both physical and emotional closeness, creating a sense of connection that goes beyond the surface. It is a cornerstone of a healthy marriage, providing partners with a safe space to express vulnerability, share experiences, and deepen their understanding of each other.

6.2 Navigating Physical Intimacy

Physical intimacy is a powerful expression of love and desire within a marriage. As couples transition from dating to marriage, maintaining a fulfilling and satisfying physical connection becomes essential. Partners should openly communicate their preferences, explore each other's needs, and prioritize creating an environment that fosters intimacy.

6.3 Cultivating Emotional Intimacy

Emotional intimacy involves sharing one's inner thoughts, feelings, and vulnerabilities. It requires a foundation of trust, empathy, and active listening. Couples can cultivate emotional intimacy by engaging in deep conversations, showing appreciation for each other, and consistently demonstrating care and support.

6.4 Prioritizing Quality Time

Quality time is a key ingredient in nurturing both physical and emotional intimacy. Amid the busyness of life, carving out moments to connect on a meaningful level strengthens the bond between partners. This can include activities that bring joy, shared hobbies, or simply spending quiet moments together.

6.5 Communicating Love Languages

Understanding and expressing each other's love languages is a potent way to foster intimacy. Whether through words of affirmation, acts of service, quality time, physical touch, or receiving gifts, aligning with each other's love languages helps partners feel valued and understood.

6.6 Managing External Factors

Various external factors can impact intimacy, from stress and work-related pressures to health issues. Couples should be attuned to these factors and work together to minimize their impact. Open communication about challenges and seeking support when needed contributes to maintaining intimacy.

6.7 Embracing Change and Evolution

Intimacy evolves over time as individuals and the relationship itself change. Couples should be prepared to adapt and discover new ways to connect as they navigate life's different stages. Embracing change with an open heart ensures that intimacy remains a dynamic and evolving aspect of the relationship.

6.8 Seeking Professional Help

If intimacy challenges persist, seeking the guidance of a therapist or counselor can be beneficial. Professionals can provide insights, techniques, and strategies to address obstacles and revitalize intimacy.

By nurturing both physical and emotional intimacy, couples strengthen the bond that holds their marriage together. Prioritizing quality time, effective communication, and understanding each other's needs helps maintain a vibrant and fulfilling connection. Intimacy is not just an aspect of marriage; it is the fuel that keeps the flame of love burning brightly, creating a partnership that thrives on shared experiences, trust, and a deep emotional connection.

7

Balancing Independence and Togetherness

In the intricate dance of marriage, finding the delicate balance between individuality and togetherness is an art worth mastering. This chapter delves into the significance of preserving personal identities while nurturing a thriving partnership. We will explore techniques that help couples strike the right equilibrium between personal space and quality time together.

7.1 The Duality of Identity

Marriage merges two distinct individuals into a shared journey, but it's essential to remember that each person retains their own identity. Preserving individuality within the context of a partnership enhances self-esteem, personal growth, and contributes to the richness of the relationship.

7.2 Fostering Personal Growth

Maintaining independence allows each partner to pursue personal passions, goals, and interests. This pursuit of growth not only benefits the individual but also enriches the partnership by bringing new experiences, insights, and energy into the relationship.

7.3 The Art of Compromise

Balancing independence and togetherness requires a willingness to compromise and communicate openly. Partners should discuss their expectations for personal space and quality time together. Finding common ground ensures that both individuals' needs are met.

7.4 Establishing Boundaries

Clear and respectful boundaries help partners navigate personal space within the context of the relationship. These boundaries might involve setting aside designated alone time or communicating preferences for social engagements. Establishing and respecting boundaries fosters a sense of safety and trust.

7.5 Quality over Quantity

In the pursuit of a balanced relationship, the quality of time spent together often matters more than the quantity. Focusing on meaningful interactions rather than constant togetherness allows couples to enjoy shared experiences without feeling suffocated.

7.6 Pursuing Shared and Individual Interests

Couples can strike a balance by participating in activities they enjoy together while also pursuing individual interests. This approach allows for shared experiences as well as opportunities to thrive independently.

7.7 Honoring Communication

Open and honest communication is the cornerstone of balancing independence and togetherness. Partners should discuss their preferences, concerns, and aspirations. Regular check-ins ensure that both individuals are aligned and satisfied with the balance they've struck.

7.8 Embracing Flexibility

The balance between independence and togetherness is not fixed; it evolves over time. As life circumstances change, couples should be flexible and adjust their approach accordingly. This adaptability ensures that the balance remains harmonious and in sync with the couple's evolving needs.

By maintaining individual identities while nurturing a strong partnership, couples create a marriage that thrives on mutual support, respect, and shared experiences. Finding the balance between personal space and time together enhances both partners' growth, self-esteem, and overall well-being. Through open communication, boundaries, and a commitment to compromise, couples can create a relationship that is both deeply fulfilling and beautifully balanced.

8

Dealing with Family and In-Laws

The tapestry of marriage is woven not only from the threads of the couple's relationship but also from the intricate connections with extended families. This chapter delves into the complexities of managing relationships with in-laws and extended family members. We will explore strategies for setting healthy boundaries, effective communication, and maintaining harmony within the broader family context.

8.1 The Impact of Extended Families

Marriage often brings together not just two individuals, but two families with their own dynamics, traditions, and expectations. Navigating these relationships requires sensitivity, understanding, and a commitment to fostering positive interactions.

8.2 Setting Boundaries

Healthy boundaries are essential for preserving the couple's autonomy and protecting their relationship. Couples should openly discuss and establish boundaries that define their personal space, time, and decisions. Clear boundaries help prevent undue interference and maintain a sense of independence.

8.3 Open Communication

Communication plays a pivotal role in managing relationships with in-laws and extended family members. Partners should openly share their feelings, expectations, and concerns. Regular conversations can prevent misunderstandings and create an environment of mutual understanding.

8.4 Defusing Conflicts

Conflict is a natural part of any relationship, and interactions with extended family members can sometimes lead to disagreements. When conflicts arise, it's important for partners to address them calmly, respectfully, and without placing blame. Seeking resolution rather than escalation promotes harmony.

8.5 United Front

Presenting a united front as a couple can help navigate potentially challenging situations. Partners should stand together and communicate decisions jointly, demonstrating a shared commitment to each other's well-being and the relationship.

8.6 Acknowledging Differences

Cultural, generational, and personality differences can lead to misunderstandings. Partners should acknowledge these differences and approach them with empathy and respect. Embracing diversity can enrich the relationship and the interactions with extended family members.

8.7 Creating Traditions

Couples can create their own traditions that integrate elements from both sides of the family. Establishing unique rituals helps foster a sense of unity and allows partners to honor their individual backgrounds.

8.8 Seeking External Support

If managing relationships with extended family becomes particularly challenging, seeking the guidance of a therapist or counselor can be valuable. Professionals can provide insights and techniques to navigate complex family dynamics and maintain a harmonious partnership.

By skillfully managing relationships with extended family members and in-laws, couples enrich the fabric of their marriage. Setting boundaries, practicing open communication, and navigating conflicts with grace contribute to a balanced and harmonious family ecosystem. Through mutual respect and a commitment to maintaining the sanctity of their partnership, couples create a foundation that can withstand the complexities and challenges of interwoven family dynamics.

9

Handling Life Transitions

Marriage is a journey marked by twists, turns, and significant life transitions. This chapter delves into the intricacies of navigating major changes that impact the early years of marriage, such as career shifts, relocations, or other significant life events. We will explore how couples can approach these transitions as a united team, fostering resilience and growth within their partnership.

9.1 The Nature of Life Transitions

Life transitions, whether anticipated or unexpected, have a profound impact on a marriage. Changes such as career shifts, moving, or major life events challenge couples to adapt, communicate, and grow together. Approaching these transitions with a united front is essential for weathering the changes successfully.

9.2 Embracing Flexibility

Flexibility is a key attribute during times of transition. Couples should be open to change, willing to adjust their plans, and able to adapt their routines. A flexible mindset helps partners navigate the uncertainties that transitions often bring.

9.3 Communicating Openly

Transparent and honest communication becomes paramount during life transitions. Partners should share their thoughts, concerns, and hopes openly, ensuring that they are on the same page and able to make informed decisions together.

9.4 Supporting Each Other's Goals

Transitions often involve pursuing new opportunities or making sacrifices for the benefit of the partnership. Couples should actively support each other's goals and dreams, providing the encouragement and understanding needed during periods of change.

9.5 Mutual Decision-Making

In navigating life transitions, decisions should be made jointly. Partners should collaboratively assess their options, weigh the pros and cons, and make choices that align with their shared goals and values.

9.6 Managing Stress

Life transitions can be stressful, and managing stress is crucial for maintaining a healthy partnership. Couples should prioritize self-care, engage in stress-reduction techniques, and find ways to support each other's emotional well-being.

9.7 Seeking External Support

If the challenges of a life transition become overwhelming, seeking the guidance of a therapist or counselor can be valuable. Professionals can offer coping strategies, communication techniques, and insights to navigate the changes successfully.

9.8 Celebrating Milestones

Amidst the challenges of life transitions, couples should also take time to celebrate their milestones and achievements. Marking moments of growth and progress reinforces the sense of unity and accomplishment within the partnership.

By approaching major life transitions as a united team, couples can navigate change with resilience, grace, and mutual support. Flexibility, transparent communication, and a commitment to each other's well-being help partners weather the challenges that transitions bring. Ultimately, these shared experiences contribute to the depth and strength of the partnership, allowing couples to grow individually and together while embracing the evolving landscape of their marriage.

10

Conflict Resolution Strategies

Conflict is an inevitable aspect of any relationship, including marriage. This chapter delves into the art of resolving conflicts in the early years of marriage, highlighting effective approaches that promote understanding, compromise, and the pursuit of win-win solutions. By mastering these strategies, couples can navigate conflicts with grace and strengthen their partnership.

10.1 The Nature of Conflict

Conflict arises from differences in opinions, preferences, and expectations. In the context of marriage, addressing conflicts with a positive mindset can lead to growth, improved communication, and a deeper understanding of each other.

10.2 Active Listening

Active listening is a cornerstone of conflict resolution. Partners should listen attentively to each other's perspectives without interrupting or formulating responses. This practice demonstrates respect and encourages empathy.

10.3 Expressing Feelings Calmly

During conflicts, expressing feelings in a calm and respectful manner is essential. Using "I" statements to communicate concerns and emotions avoids blame and creates an atmosphere of open dialogue.

10.4 Identifying Core Issues

Often, conflicts are symptomatic of deeper underlying issues. Couples should work together to identify the root causes of their disagreements, which enables them to address the core concerns effectively.

10.5 Finding Common Ground

Focusing on shared goals and interests helps partners find common ground. By identifying areas of agreement, couples lay the foundation for collaborative problem-solving.

10.6 Seeking Win-Win Solutions

Striving for win-win solutions benefits both partners and the relationship as a whole. Rather than seeking to "win" the argument, couples should collaborate to find resolutions that meet both individuals' needs.

10.7 Taking Breaks

Sometimes conflicts become heated, and taking a break can be beneficial. Couples should agree on a time to revisit the discussion after cooling down, allowing for a more productive exchange of ideas.

10.8 Practicing Empathy

Empathy is a powerful tool in conflict resolution. Partners should strive to understand each other's viewpoints, emotions, and concerns. This practice fosters a sense of connection and helps de-escalate conflicts.

10.9 Using Humor

Applying humor in conflict resolution can diffuse tension and create a more lighthearted atmosphere. However, humor should be used with caution and respect to avoid trivializing important issues.

10.10 Seeking Professional Help

If conflicts persist or become increasingly challenging to resolve, seeking the assistance of a therapist or counselor can be invaluable. Professionals provide techniques and insights to address complex issues constructively.

By embracing these conflict resolution strategies, couples can transform conflicts into opportunities for growth, understanding, and increased intimacy. Approaching disagreements with active listening, empathy, and a commitment to finding win-win solutions allows partners to navigate challenges with respect and grace. Ultimately, mastering these techniques contributes to a strong and resilient partnership that thrives on effective communication and mutual support.

11

Fostering Mutual Growth

Marriage is not only a union of hearts but also a catalyst for personal and relational growth. This chapter delves into the concept of fostering mutual growth in the early years of marriage, emphasizing the importance of supporting each other's individual development while nurturing the partnership itself.

11.1 The Journey of Growth
Marriage provides a unique platform for personal and relational growth. As individuals embark on this journey together, they have the opportunity to evolve, learn, and flourish both as individuals and as a couple.

11.2 Supporting Individual Aspirations
Partners should actively encourage each other's personal aspirations, goals, and dreams. This support can manifest through offering encouragement, celebrating achievements, and providing a safe space to explore new endeavors.

11.3 Celebrating Milestones
Recognizing and celebrating personal milestones contributes to a sense of accomplishment and pride. Whether achieving professional goals, pursuing

hobbies, or taking steps towards personal development, these milestones enrich both the individual and the partnership.

11.4 Navigating Change Together

As individuals grow and evolve, their needs and interests may change. Couples should navigate these changes together, embracing each other's transformations and adapting to the shifting landscape of their relationship.

11.5 Balancing Individual and Shared Goals

Finding the balance between individual and shared goals is key to fostering mutual growth. Partners should work together to ensure that their personal aspirations align with the overall trajectory of the relationship.

11.6 Communication and Feedback

Open communication plays a pivotal role in mutual growth. Partners should engage in regular conversations about their individual journeys, share insights, and provide constructive feedback that promotes personal development.

11.7 Encouraging Learning and Exploration

Partners should encourage each other to engage in continuous learning and exploration. This might involve reading, attending workshops, or pursuing new experiences that contribute to personal enrichment.

11.8 Embracing Change and Adaptation

Mutual growth requires an open-minded approach to change and adaptation. Partners should be willing to evolve alongside each other, even if it means stepping out of their comfort zones.

11.9 Respecting Boundaries

While supporting each other's growth is important, respecting individual boundaries is equally essential. Partners should recognize that personal growth journeys may involve certain areas that are private and not meant to be shared.

11.10 Reflecting on Progress

Couples should periodically reflect on their individual and shared growth. This reflection helps partners appreciate the progress they've made, acknowledge challenges overcome, and set new intentions for the future.

By fostering mutual growth, couples create a partnership that thrives on shared aspirations, personal achievements, and continuous learning. Encouraging each other's individual development strengthens the bond between partners and contributes to the depth and richness of the relationship. Through open communication, support, and a commitment to evolving together, couples lay the foundation for a marriage that not only withstands the test of time but also flourishes as both individuals and as a united team.

12

Celebrating Milestones and Looking Forward

As couples embark on the journey of marriage, the early years mark a period of discovery, growth, and shared experiences. This chapter reflects on this transformative phase, highlighting key takeaways and offering guidance for continuing to build a strong foundation for a lasting partnership.

12.1 Reflecting on the Journey

Looking back on the early years of marriage allows couples to appreciate the distance they've traveled. Reflecting on the challenges overcome, the joys shared, and the growth experienced provides a sense of accomplishment and gratitude.

12.2 Celebrating Milestones

Celebrating milestones is an opportunity to acknowledge the progress made as a couple. Whether it's marking the first year of marriage, buying a home, or achieving personal goals, these celebrations reinforce the unity and bond between partners.

12.3 Embracing Change and Adaptation

The early years of marriage are marked by change and adaptation. Couples should embrace the flexibility that comes with navigating new roles, responsibilities, and challenges. Embracing change together fosters resilience and deepens the partnership.

12.4 Prioritizing Communication

Effective communication remains essential throughout the journey of marriage. Partners should continue to communicate openly, actively listening to each other's needs, concerns, and aspirations. Communication maintains the connection and understanding that underpin the relationship.

12.5 Nurturing Intimacy

Intimacy, both physical and emotional, remains integral to the marriage. Couples should continue to prioritize quality time, shared experiences, and open conversations that deepen their connection and keep the flame of love alive.

12.6 Pursuing Individual Growth

As the years pass, individual growth should remain a priority. Partners should continue to pursue personal goals, interests, and hobbies that contribute to their well-being and, by extension, the strength of the relationship.

12.7 Setting New Goals

Continually setting new goals as a couple maintains a sense of purpose and direction. From personal aspirations to shared dreams, setting goals keeps the partnership dynamic and encourages ongoing growth.

12.8 Seeking Support

Throughout the marriage journey, seeking support when needed is valuable. Whether through couples' counseling, mentorship, or engaging with a strong social network, external guidance provides insights and perspectives that enhance the partnership.

12.9 Embracing Gratitude

Practicing gratitude for each other and the journey of marriage is a powerful way to sustain a positive outlook. Expressing appreciation for the small and significant moments fosters a sense of contentment and reinforces the bond between partners.

12.10 Looking Forward

As couples move beyond the early years of marriage, they do so with a foundation built on shared experiences, open communication, and mutual support. Looking forward to the future with optimism, determination, and a commitment to continuing to build upon this foundation ensures a marriage that thrives in every season of life.

In celebrating milestones and looking ahead, couples reaffirm their dedication to a partnership characterized by growth, understanding, and enduring love. By reflecting on their journey, embracing change, and maintaining the principles that have guided them, couples ensure that their early years of marriage serve as the foundation for a lifetime of shared happiness and connection.

Conclusion

As the curtain falls on this exploration of the early years of marriage, we are reminded of the profound significance of laying a solid foundation for a partnership that stands the test of time. The journey you embark upon as a couple is not merely a sequence of events; it is an opportunity to craft a meaningful and enduring connection.

Throughout this book, we have delved into the intricacies of building a strong foundation in the early years of marriage. From communication to conflict resolution, from intimacy to individual growth, each chapter has offered insights and strategies to guide you on this transformative path.

BUILDING A STRONG FOUNDATION: THE EARLY YEARS OF MARRIAGE

The importance of approaching your marriage with intention, commitment, and a dedication to mutual growth cannot be overstated. These early years set the tone for the journey ahead. The decisions you make, the habits you establish, and the love you nurture during this time shape the trajectory of your partnership.

As you navigate life's challenges, celebrate milestones, and explore new horizons together, remember that the process of building a strong foundation is ongoing. Continue to communicate openly, support each other's aspirations, and prioritize the well-being of your relationship. Embrace change with an open heart, adapt with flexibility, and never underestimate the power of shared experiences.

The pages of this book merely scratch the surface of the complexities and joys that marriage brings. Your journey will undoubtedly have its own unique twists and turns. The key lies in approaching each day with the intention to learn, grow, and deepen your connection.

May your marriage be a testament to the beauty of love, partnership, and shared growth. As you move forward hand in hand, may you find joy in every triumph, strength in every challenge, and the unwavering support of a partner who walks beside you through every chapter of this remarkable journey called marriage.

www.ingramcontent.com/pod-product-compliance
Lightning Source LLC
LaVergne TN
LVHW010440070526
838199LV00066B/6107